Stark County District Library
www.StarkLibrary.org
330.452.0665

W9-ALM-965

Liberty Rising

The Story of the Statue of Liberty

DISCARDED

For my children, Deirdre Vincena Shea and Thomas Sullivan Shea

—*P. D. S.*

*To all those who have bravely uprooted themselves from around the world
to find their way to this wonderful land*

—*W. Z.*

Liberty Rising

The Story of the Statue of Liberty

PEGI DEITZ SHEA

illustrated by WADE ZAHARES

SQUARE
FISH

Henry Holt and Company ✦ New York

AUTHOR'S NOTE

Constructing a building fifteen stories high is a hard job. Architects must make sure a building will serve the people using it for tens, maybe hundreds of years. Today architects have many tools to help them—computers, powerful construction equipment, and strong, flexible materials.

Let's go back to the year 1875, before most people used electricity and when telephones were just invented. Before cars and well before computers. Imagine designing and building a monument fifteen stories high, unbuilding and shipping it in parts across an ocean, and then reconstructing the monument in another country. Using wood, plaster, leaf-thin copper, and rivets, the sculptor Frédéric-Auguste Bartholdi and his crew did just that. They created a work of art, the Statue of Liberty, and she still thrills and inspires the millions who gaze upon her every day.

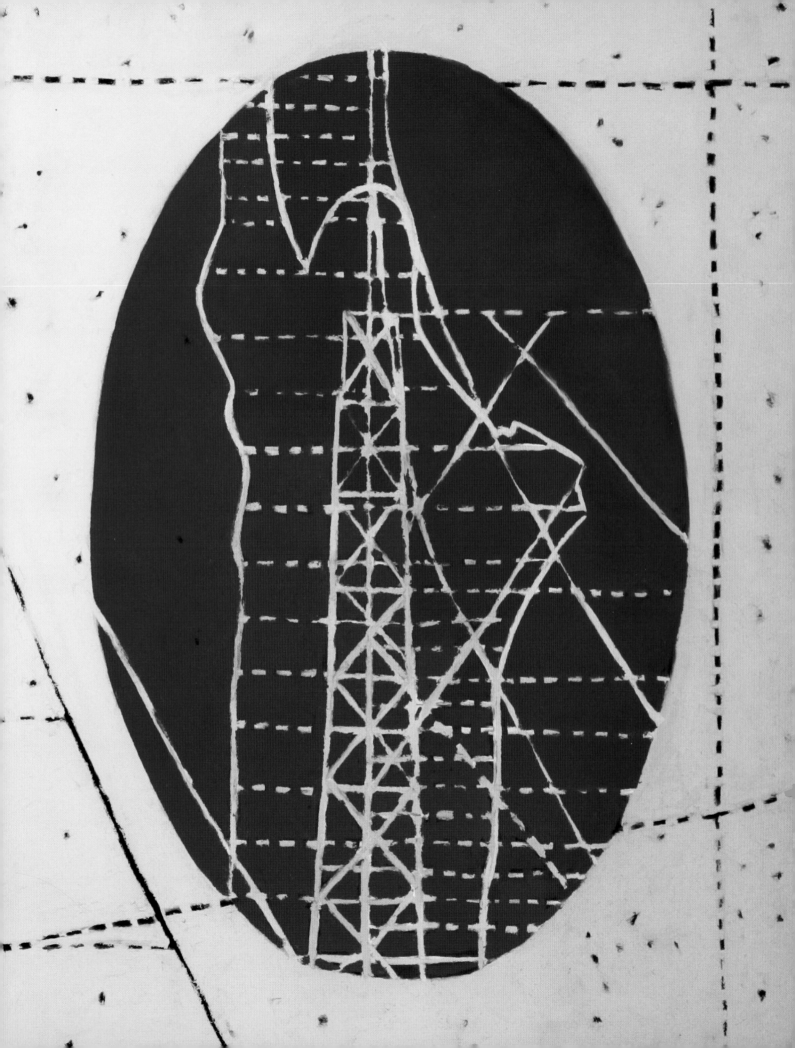

Have you ever watched a house, an office, or a store being built? They're all constructed from the inside out. That's how the Statue of Liberty was made. In fact, the Statue of Liberty was built several times.

The idea for a spectacular monument was born inside the heart of Edouard de Laboulaye, a French law professor. He had studied the U.S. Constitution in great detail and longed for a similar government in France. For America's hundredth birthday on July 4, 1876, Laboulaye hoped to create a magnificent gift that represented freedom. After all, France had helped American colonists win their independence in 1776, and the countries had remained allies.

Laboulaye viewed this monument as a gift from one people to another—not from one government to another. He would not ask for funding from the French government, which was still suffering from many years of war in Europe. Instead, he would ask for donations from the French and American people who shared "a fraternity of feelings, a community of efforts." Laboulaye set up the Franco-American Union, which collected 200,000 francs in its first year. The union held lotteries and banquets and sold miniature monuments to raise money. Adults and children all across France sent contributions for the worthy cause.

Frédéric-Auguste Bartholdi grew excited about his friend Laboulaye's worthy cause. Bartholdi enjoyed creating large works of art. He drew inspiration from visiting the towering yet elegant classic buildings of Greece and Italy and the immense pyramids and the Sphinx of Egypt. Paintings of the Colossus of Rhodes—a lighthouse statue, and one of the Seven Wonders of the Ancient World—fascinated him. Only recently, Bartholdi had designed a similar lighthouse monument for the newly built Suez Canal. Despite its fancy name, *Egypt Bringing the Light to Asia*, the torch-bearing statue was never built. Bartholdi would now get another chance.

With Laboulaye's encouragement, Bartholdi began sketching and making models in 1870. He gave the female statue a face resembling his mother's, and draped the statue in classic robes similar to those worn by his *Egypt*. Bartholdi also wanted his creation to honor the Colossus of Rhodes. So he featured two important images—a raised torch and a crown of seven rays, standing for the seven seas and the seven continents.

When Bartholdi traveled to America in 1871 to raise money for the monument, he happened upon Liberty's future site. He sailed into New York Harbor and passed by Bedloe's Island. The old fort—Fort Wood—on the island did not impress him. But the island's location seemed perfect! Liberty should shine there, Bartholdi decided, where she could welcome all to America. And unlike the Colossus of Rhodes, crumpled by an earthquake after only fifty years, this colossus would be built to last.

Once back in France, Bartholdi continued working on various designs. He built small models of Liberty to test his ideas. Would the statue hold anything besides a torch? In later models, he added the tablet Liberty cradles in her left arm. Keeping with the classic theme, Bartholdi had "July 4, 1776" etched in Roman numerals on the tablet. He put a broken chain around her ankle to show freedom from bonds. How big could the statue be without toppling over in a natural disaster? Bartholdi determined 151 feet. A pedestal and base built on site by Americans would make the statue twice as high. Bartholdi had to be sure Liberty could stand up to storms.

In August 1875, Bartholdi unveiled the first complete scale model of *Liberty Enlightening the World*. The clay structure—only a bit more than four feet high—stood proudly enough to win approval by the Franco-American Union.

Soon, Liberty grew in scale as Bartholdi tested her strength. It would have been foolish to think that what worked with a four-foot model would also work at 151 feet. For example, Bartholdi had to bring the right arm closer to the statue's head. The new position would keep it safer from wind, and it could be better supported by the main structure.

So Bartholdi and his team built a plaster model nine and a half feet tall—almost as high as a basketball hoop. Then they made and studied another model exactly four times as high—at thirty-eight feet, the height of a three-story building.

Continuing upward, they constructed a model nearly four times higher again to reach 151 feet, the size of the actual statue. If Liberty were to lie down, she would stretch half the length of a football field. Bartholdi used this final plaster model to make measurements and frames for the statue's "skin," or outer layers.

Many spectators in France and America paid money to see parts of Liberty before she was put together. In his studio, Bartholdi and his team created the statue's most memorable and symbolic sections first: the head and the hand holding the torch. Bartholdi himself traveled with the right hand and torch to Philadelphia for America's hundredth birthday celebration in 1876. The hand and torch were then displayed in New York City. All the while, Bartholdi helped American business leaders raise money for the base and pedestal. Back in France, Liberty's head took a hayride on its way to the 1878 World's Fair in Paris. People could climb inside and peer out from the crown.

Bartholdi wanted Liberty completed before 1900, so he needed many more craftsmen. He hired the coppersmiths of Gaget, Gauthier and Company, which also provided a new and larger work space. Bartholdi chose copper for Liberty's skin because this inexpensive metal lasted a long time. At about an eighth of an inch thick, it also bent easily. Workers shaped the sheets of copper by hammering them from the inside out. This technique is called "repoussé." The copper sheets became puzzle pieces to form Liberty's body, tablet, and torch. More than 300,000 rivets hold the copper sheets together.

While the workers pounded away at the copper, Alexandre-Gustave Eiffel (who later designed the Eiffel Tower) built a freestanding iron skeleton for Liberty. Diagonal braces connected the iron bars for extra support. The copper skin grew upward from her toes around this skeleton; a staircase stood in for a spine. The only entrance into the statue was a door on the sole of her right sandal.

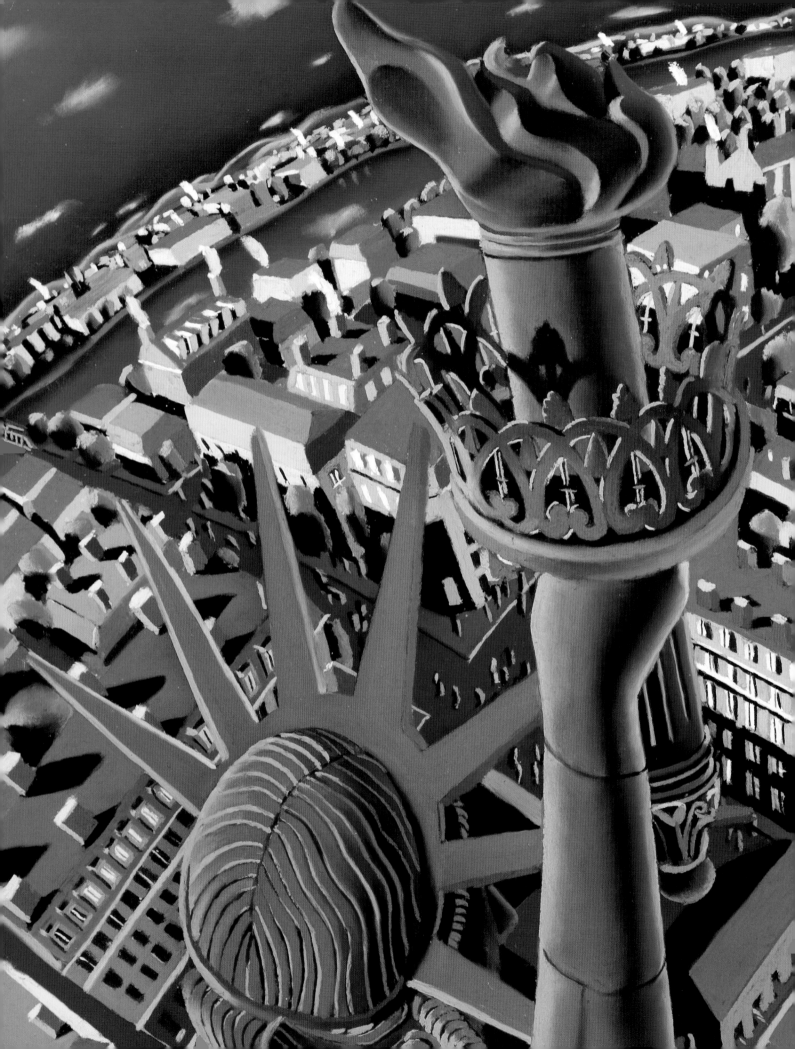

Soon Liberty dwarfed the homes and shops of the Paris neighborhood. Bartholdi predicted, "Next spring one will see it overlook the entire city." Merchants put up with the noise because Liberty brought onlookers to the area, and onlookers became customers.

On the Fourth of July in 1884, Bartholdi and French leaders presented *Liberty Enlightening the World* to American ambassadors in Paris. Sadly, the man who had first dreamed of this grand monument was absent. Edouard de Laboulaye had died in 1883. Imagine, though, the pride and delight he would have felt seeing children and adults peer out from Liberty's crown and knowing that they shared his vision of freedom.

Having spent years building Liberty, Bartholdi and his workers now had to *unbuild* the statue. Liberty needed to be shipped in pieces to America—there was no other way to transport a structure this size. The statue was packed up in 214 crates, then loaded into seventy train cars. The train took the crates to Rouen, where the ship *Isère* waited, for the monthlong voyage across the Atlantic Ocean.

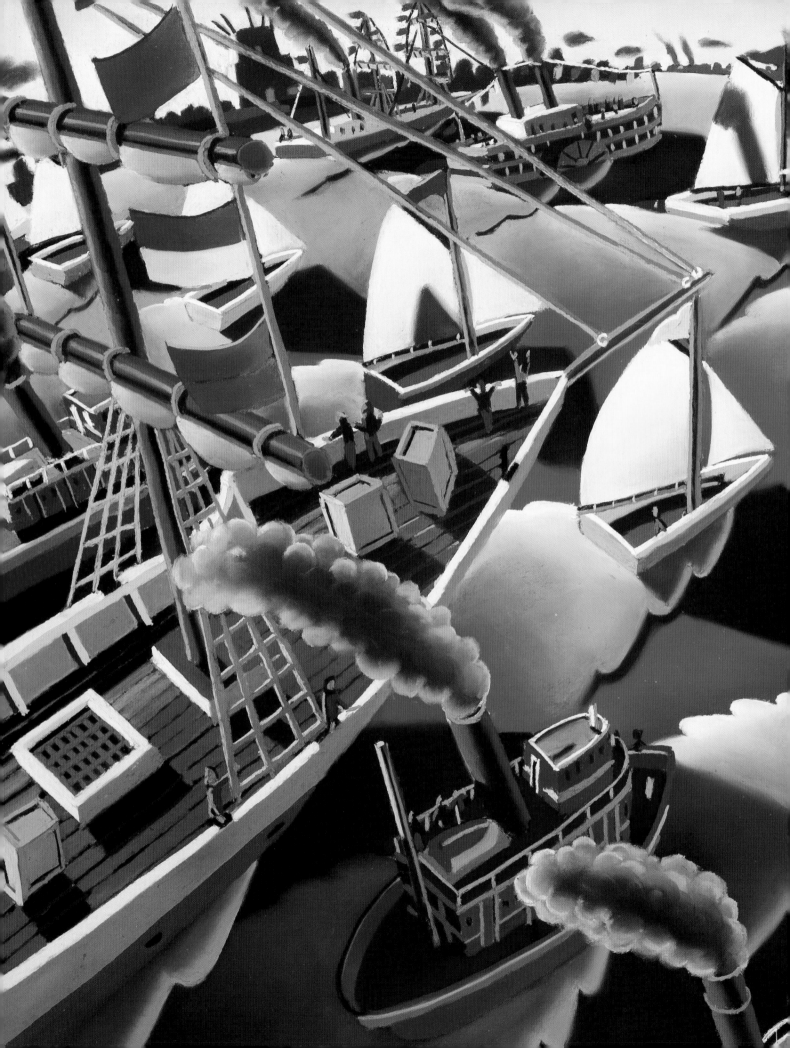

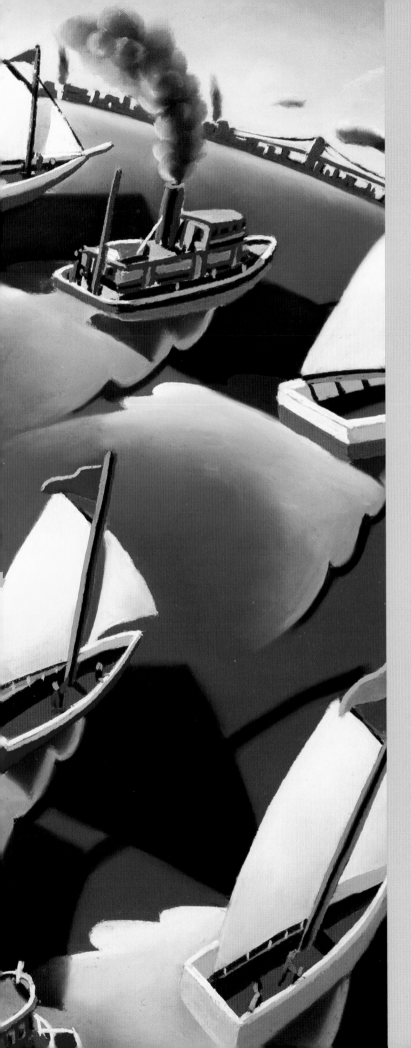

A parade of boats led the *Isère* into New York Harbor on June 17, 1885. Bartholdi expected to erect Liberty right away. Unfortunately, America hadn't yet raised enough money to finish Liberty's base and pedestal. New Yorkers, especially, had been distracted by the prolonged construction of the Brooklyn Bridge from 1869 to 1883. Liberty would have to wait in crates for as long as it took to pay for the pedestal.

The American architect hired to design the pedestal, Richard Morris Hunt, had to wait as well, but he didn't sit idle. Hunt had studied at the École des Beaux-Arts in Paris, and he was in high demand for his fancy French Renaissance style. Most famous for building one of New York's first skyscrapers, the Tribune Building, in 1875, he also built a castlelike home on Fifth Avenue for the wealthy Vanderbilt family, as well as the Parisian-style apartment building, the Stuyvesant. Bartholdi and Hunt wrote each other letters regularly throughout the pedestal design process.

To speed the fund-raising, newspaper publisher Joseph Pulitzer began printing the name of every person who donated money. Children sent in their allowances and recent immigrants donated a day's wage. Pulitzer ran cartoons and essays teasing the wealthy who didn't contribute. Finally, the U.S. government agreed to help pay for the rebuilding and dedication of the statue. Liberty would fall under the federal category of "lighthouse."

Construction began. Like the foundation of a house, the base was a wide concrete mass partly sunk into the ground. The outer area of the base aboveground would be used by visitors and staff. The decorative yet sturdy pedestal was designed to hold Liberty high. Behind the pedestal's classic friezes and columns, concrete and steel girders connected to the statue. Once the base and pedestal were completed in the spring of 1886, it took six months to rebuild Liberty on top of it. Special copper rods ran down inside the statue and pedestal into the ground, protecting Liberty from lightning. There were 392 steps installed to lead visitors all the way up to the torch on top.

Bartholdi himself unveiled *Liberty Enlightening the World* on October 28, 1886. Joining him to dedicate the statue were President Grover Cleveland, the pedestal architect Hunt, the chief fund-raisers, and others from both France and America. Hundreds of spectators in boats gazed up at Liberty's face while cannon salutes cut through the drizzle and clouds. Standing at the foot of the highest structure—305 feet tall—ever built by man at that time, Bartholdi said, "The dream of my life is accomplished."

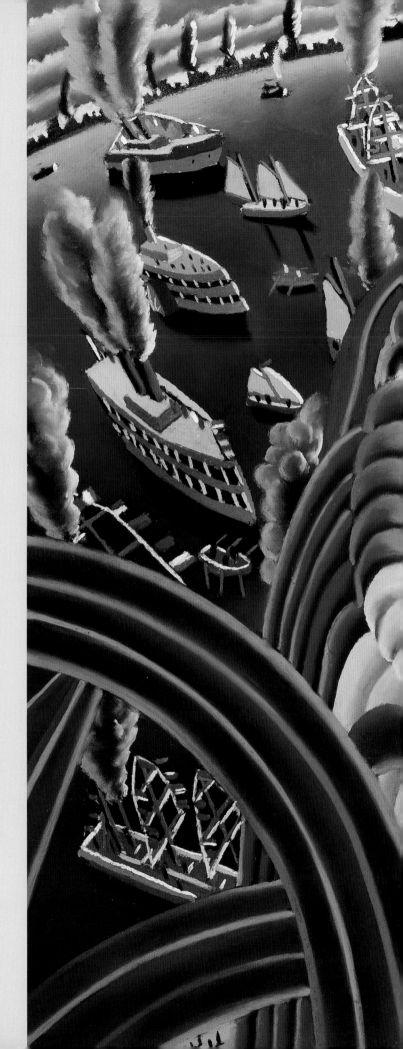

The Statue

Open here →

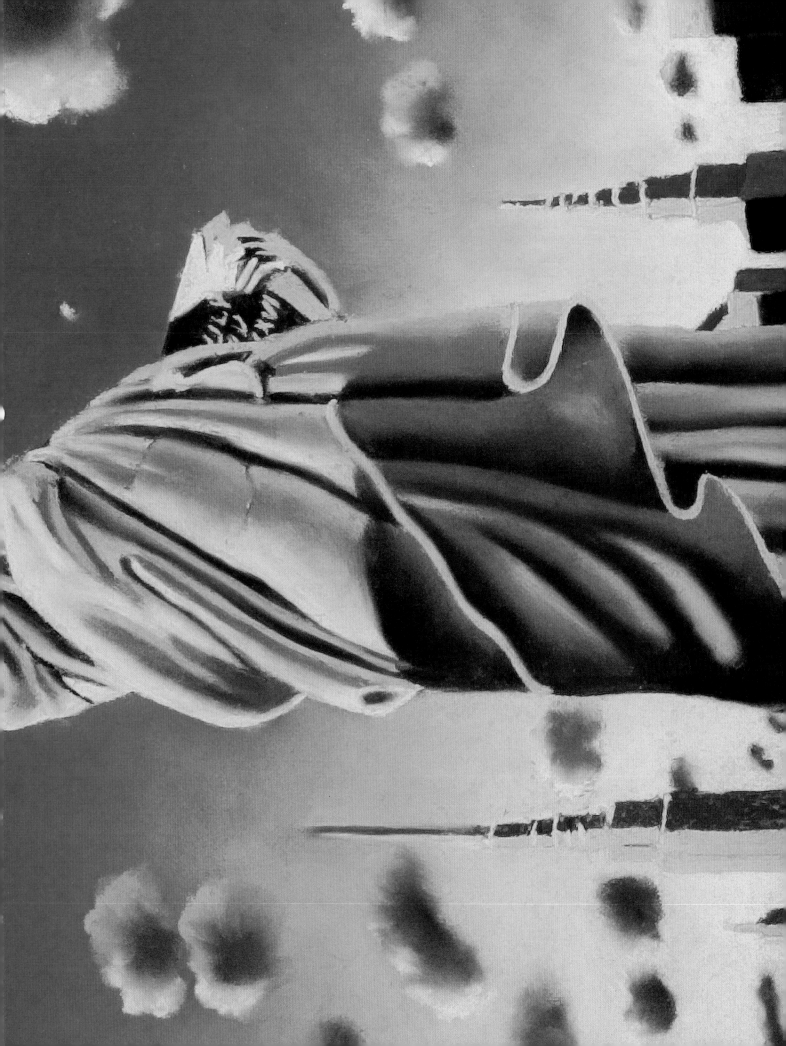

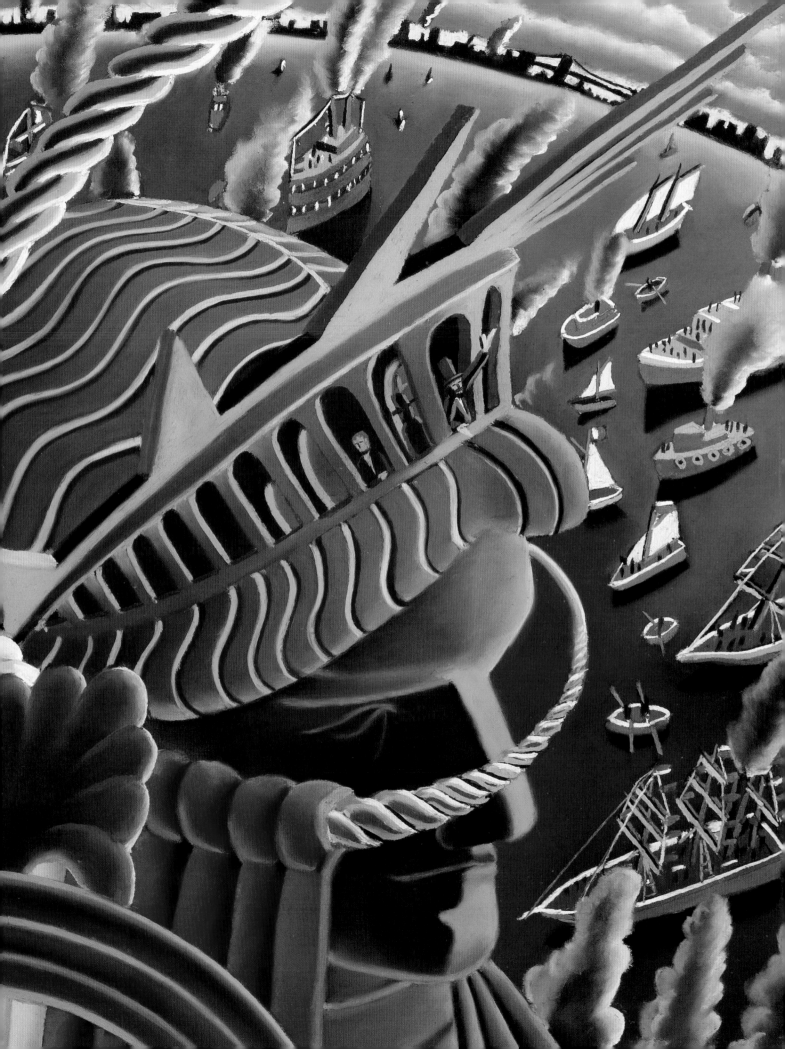

# of Liberty

← Open here

The dream of many people is to breathe free. The Statue of Liberty represents this dream. Let her inspire the world to give and to cherish the gift of freedom.

"... *From her beacon-hand*
Glows world-wide welcome ..."

—from "The New Colossus,"
by Emma Lazarus, 1883

MORE INTERESTING FACTS ABOUT THE LIFE OF LIBERTY

1871—During his first American visit, Bartholdi met President Ulysses S. Grant, Massachusetts Senator Charles Sumner, and poet Henry Wadsworth Longfellow. He also met Jeanne-Émilie Baheux de Puysieux, whom he married in 1876.

1876—America's Centennial Exhibition in Philadelphia also featured the Bartholdi Fountain. It weighed forty tons, stood thirty feet high, and featured eleven-foot-tall female nymphs. The fountain can now be enjoyed in Bartholdi Park, near the U.S. Botanic Gardens in Washington, D.C. Another work by Bartholdi in Washington is *Allegory of Africa*, a bronze sculpture in the National Gallery of Art. Bartholdi's statue of the Marquis de Lafayette still stands in Union Square Park, in New York City.

1883—Emma Lazarus wrote the poem "The New Colossus," with its famous words:

> *Not like the brazen giant of Greek fame*
> *With conquering limbs astride from land to land;*
> *Here at our sea-washed, sunset gates shall stand*
> *A mighty woman with a torch, whose flame*
> *Is the imprisoned lightning, and her name*
> *Mother of Exiles. From her beacon-hand*
> *Glows world-wide welcome; her mild eyes command*
> *The air-bridged harbor that twin cities frame.*
> *"Keep, ancient lands, your storied pomp!" cries she,*
> *With silent lips. "Give me your tired, your poor,*
> *Your huddled masses yearning to breathe free,*
> *The wretched refuse of your teeming shore;*
> *Send these, the homeless, tempest-tost to me,*
> *I lift my lamp beside the golden door!"*

Twenty years later, a plaque of the poem was mounted on Liberty's pedestal.

1885—Americans gave Parisians a thirty-eight-foot Statue of Liberty. It still stands on the Island of the Swans in the Seine River, and another replica graces the Luxembourg Gardens.

1892—The U.S. government made neighboring Ellis Island, formerly called Gull Island and Oyster Island, the official entry station for immigrants.

1901—By now, the statue was developing its protective green patina, a thin natural coat or crust formed over time when damp air meets copper. The statue would be completely green by about 1915.

1904—Bartholdi died. He and his wife had no children.

1916—Gutzon Borglum, future designer of Mount Rushmore, rebuilt Liberty's torch with panes of glass. Nicknamed "the ugly teapot" by architects, Borglum's torch can now be seen in the monument's museum.

1924—Liberty was named a national monument, and nine years later was given to the National Park Service to administer. Also in 1924, mass immigration through Ellis Island ended, though offices there provided citizenship services until 1954.

1936—The Statue of Liberty was spruced up for its fiftieth anniversary. New iron bars replaced corroded ones, and screws replaced rivets.

1940s—During World War II, the statue acted as a Navy signal station, with sailors flashing Morse code from Liberty's crown.

1956—Bedloe's Island was renamed Liberty Island. Ellis Island became part of the Statue of Liberty National Monument and Park.